SCHIRMER'S LIBRARY OF MUSICAL CLASSICS

Vol. 272

CARL CZERNY

Op. 849

Thirty
New Studies in Technics

(Études de Mécanisme)

Preparatory to
SCHOOL OF VELOCITY, Op. 299

Edited, Revised and Fingered by
G. BUONAMICI

G. SCHIRMER, Inc.

DISTRIBUTED BY

7777 W. BLUEMOUND RD. P.O. BOX 13819 MILWAUKEE, WI 53213

Thirty New Studies in Technics.

(Trente Nouvelles Etudes de Mécanisme.)

Book I.

C. CZERNY. Op.849.

+) Also practice this study transposed a semitone higher.

11193   Printed in the U. S. A.

Molto Allegro. (♩=100.)

2.

6

Allegro non troppo. (♩=72.)
sempre legato sino alla fine

3.

11193

Allegro. (♩ = 144.)
legato

4.+)

+)It is a good plan also to transpose this exercise a semitone higher, adhering to the same fingering.

Thirty New Studies in Technics.

(Trente Nouvelles Etudes de Mécanisme.)

Book II.

C. CZERNY. Op. 849.

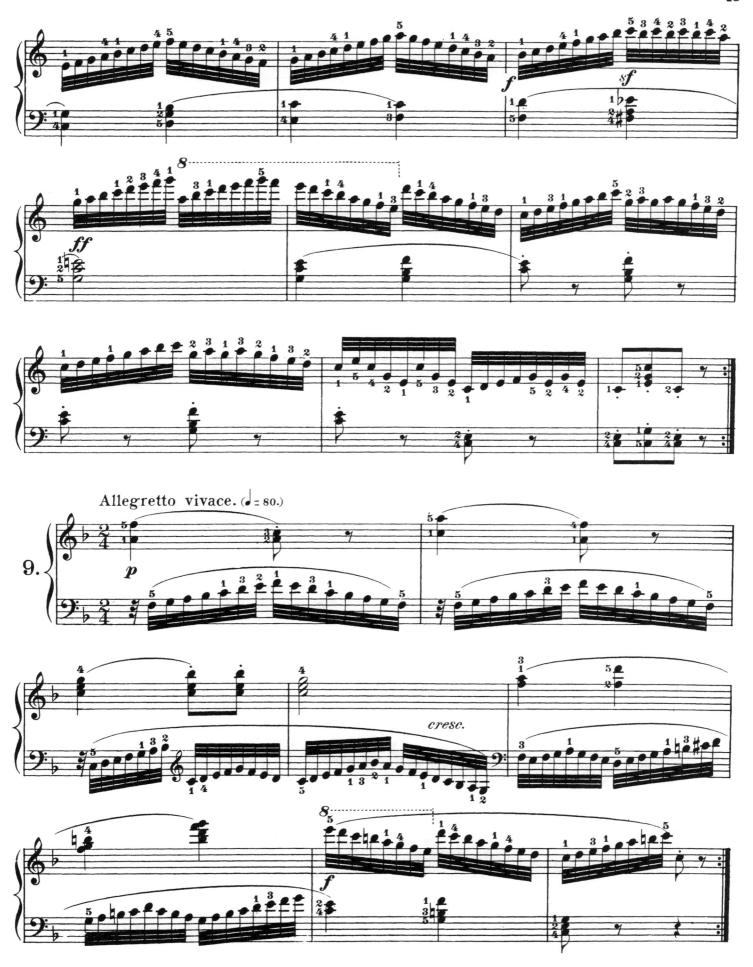

Allegretto vivace. (♩ = 80.)

9.

Allegro moderato. (♩ = 126.)

10.✝)

✝) Also practice in F♯.
41194

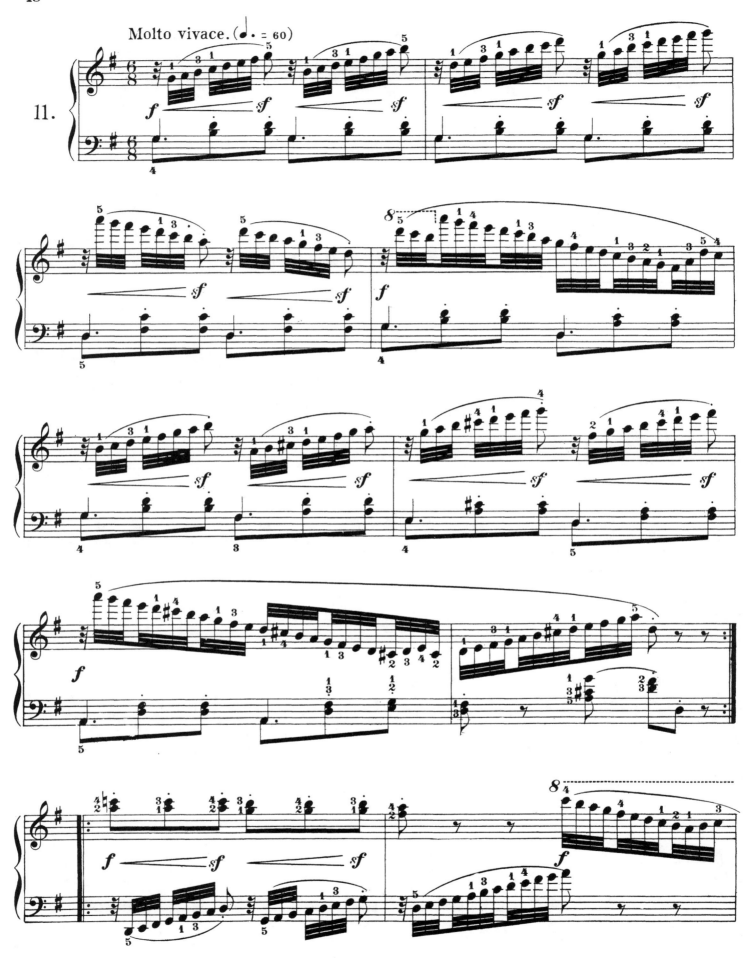

Thirty New Studies in Technics.

(Trente Nouvelles Etudes de Mécanisme.)

Book III.

C. CZERNY. Op. 849

Allegretto animato. ($\flat$ = 80.)

*) Also practice in G♭, making only indispensable changes in the fingering.

11195

Molto vivace. ($\bullet$ = 80.)

14.

Allegretto vivace. (♩ = 80.)

11195

Thirty New Studies in Technics.

Trente Nouvelles Etudes de Mécanisme.

Book IV.

C. CZERNY. Op. 849.

+) Also transpose into C♯ and C♭, retaining the fingering given.

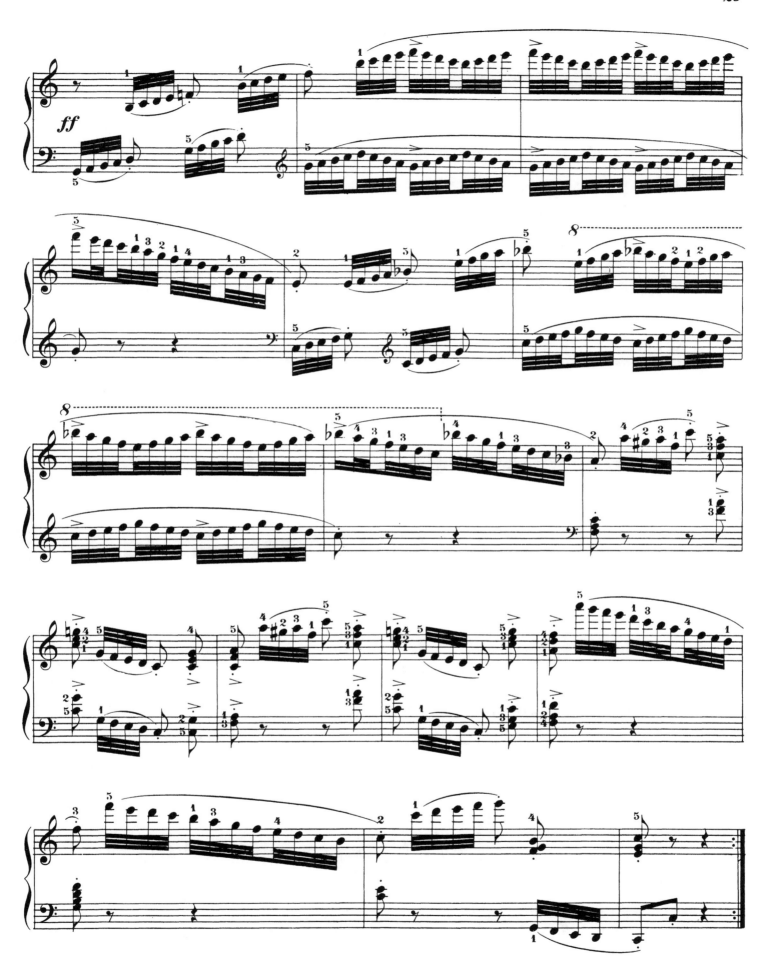

Vivace giocoso. ($\bullet$ = 108.)

17.

11196

Allegro scherzando. (♩. = 60.)

19.

p dolce leggiero.

Thirty New Studies in Technics.
(Trente Nouvelles Etudes de Mécanisme.)
Book V.

C. CZERNY. Op. 849.

11197

23.

Allegro moderato. ($\quad$ = 120.)

24.

p dolce, legato.

Thirty New Studies in Technics.

(Trentes Nouvelles Etudes de Mécanisme.)

Book VI.

C. CZERNY. Op. 849.

+) Also practice in Db, making the necessary changes in the fingering, particularly in measures 7 and 17.

48

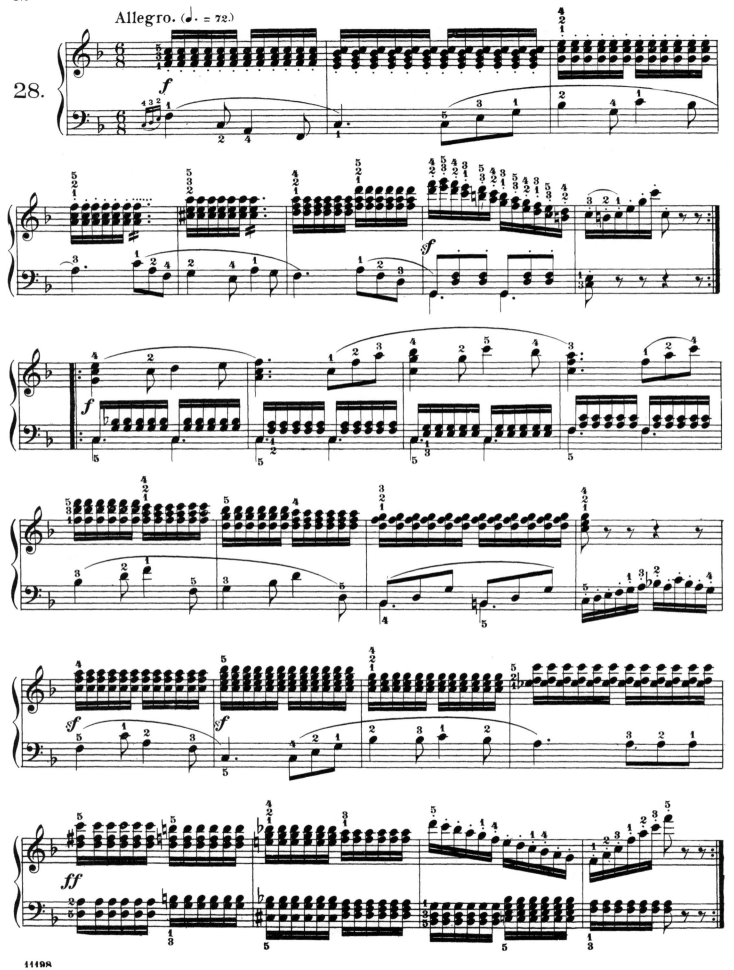

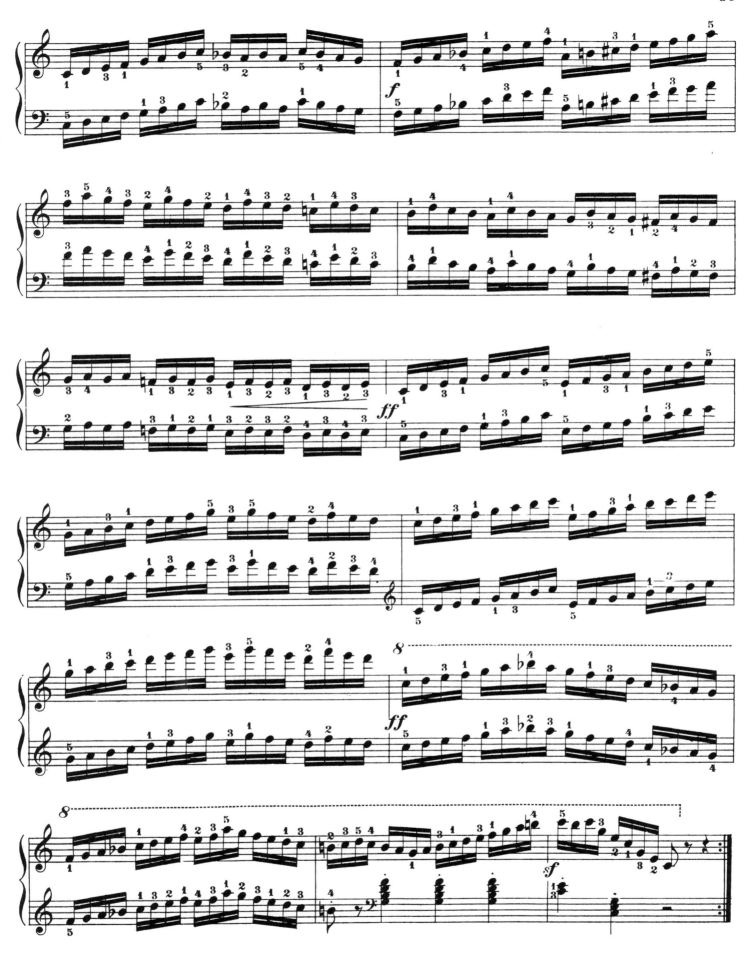